HAMPSHIRE STEAM

Scenes from ...ties

MICHAEL WELCH

Capital Transport

CONTENTS

Front cover The 'Bournemouth Belle', seen here leaving Southampton Central on 1st September 1962 behind 'Merchant Navy' Class No 35002 *Union Castle*, was without a doubt the best known and most opulent timetabled train ever to serve Hampshire. The building prominent on the horizon, one of the most famous landmarks in Hampshire, is Southampton's Civic Centre. Southampton Central Station's well known signal gantry, which was located at the end of the down platforms, is also discernible. Note that this picture shows one of the Pullman Brake coaches, which is formed immediately behind the locomotive. These very distinctive vehicles were replaced by BR Standard Full Brake coaches in the mid-1960s, thus robbing the 'Belle' of some of its character. *David Clark*

Back cover The Warwickshire Railway Society's 'Hants and Dorset' railtour, of 5th September 1965, was advertised to be hauled by an A4 Class 'Pacific' from Birmingham to Weymouth and return. At that time a number of Sir Nigel Gresley's legendary A4s survived in Scotland for working between Glasgow and Aberdeen, so the use of one of these locomotives was not entirely beyond the realms of possibility. So one can only imagine the huge disappointment felt by many of the lineside observers near Worting Junction when nothing more exciting than BR Standard Class 5 No 73085 *Melisande* heaved into view. At least the tour participants had the compensation of being hauled by an LNER-designed A1 Class Pacific from Birmingham to Banbury and by *Clun Castle* thence to Basingstoke, where No 73085 took over. *Roy Hobbs*

Overleaf At the end of the First World War the LSWR was desperately in need of a larger main line passenger locomotive, and in September 1918 the first of Robert Urie's N15 Class 4–6–0s took to the rails, an initial batch of twenty engines being constructed. The engines were principally allocated to the demanding Waterloo to Exeter services. The locomotives did not quite live up to expectations however, with poor steaming and drifting smoke being a particular source of complaints by enginemen. Various modifications were authorised by Richard Maunsell, Urie's successor, and carried out as the engines passed through Eastleigh Works. A much improved machine resulted. A further fifty-four 'King Arthurs', as the class later became known, were built during the Maunsell era and were extremely successful. They were a common sight in Hampshire from their introduction until the last example was withdrawn in late 1962. In this marvellous shot of a 'King Arthur' in full cry, a highly polished No 30791 *Sir Uwaine* is depicted near Winchfield, presumably hauling an up slow train, on 3rd January 1959. No 30791 was one of a series of these engines built by the North British Locomotive Co., Glasgow, in 1925. *Trevor Owen*

First Published 2000

ISBN 185414 229 1

Published by Capital Transport Publishing, 38 Long Elmes, Harrow Weald, Middlesex

Printed by CS Graphics, Singapore

INTRODUCTION

Hampshire is a large county which encompasses some remarkably diverse and varied countryside, ranging from huge masses of chalk downland to secluded river valleys and considerable areas of heathland. Perhaps the county's best known topographical feature is the New Forest, which has a unique and precious landscape. In addition, Hampshire also contains some of the largest conurbations in the south, including Portsmouth, with its 500 years old naval tradition, and the bustling commercial port of Southampton, best known as home to some of the world's most famous passenger liners. In steam days the popular and important holiday resort of Bournemouth was also in Hampshire, prior to the county boundary changes in 1974, and is therefore included in this album. Due to the abundance of material from the mainland, the Isle of Wight has however been omitted.

The county's railway system was no less varied than its countryside, and developed in a piecemeal fashion following the opening of the London & Southampton Railway in 1840. There were considerable contrasts between the various lines and the services they offered, perhaps the most marked being the difference between the fast, quadruple track Farnborough to Worting Junction section of the Bournemouth Line and the single track Meon Valley Line, which serviced that unspoilt, delightful, but sparsely populated area between Alton and Fareham. Towards the end, the latter line was served by a meagre service of four passenger trains each way per day, whereas on the four track Bournemouth Line it was not inconceivable for an observer to witness four trains in less than a minute! The steam trains themselves covered the whole spectrum, from the prestigious and glamorous 'Bournemouth Belle' to everyday freight trains and humble local passenger services. The lines were also remarkably varied.

Hampshire had some low lying routes that skirted the coast or ran alongside river estuaries, but it also boasted the highest railway summit in the south. This is at Medstead on the Mid Hants Line, where the railway achieves the remarkable height, by the modest standards of southern England, of 652 feet above sea level. One of the first dieselisation schemes was introduced in Hampshire in 1957 as part of BR's Modernisation Plan but, incredibly, this did not prevent the remarkable survival of steam traction on the Lymington line, which became the last steam operated passenger branch in Great Britain, lingering on until April 1967.

Despite the early encroachment of diesel multiple units on some local services, Hampshire thankfully remained a stronghold of main line steam until the inauguration of the Bournemouth Line Electrification Scheme on 10th July 1967. This ensured that the county was widely photographed in colour and it has been my pleasant task to endeavour to select the very best images, from the considerable amount of material submitted, for publication in this album. Many railway photographers have kindly delved into their collections, and as a result of this I have been able to produce an album which, I hope, provides reasonable coverage of the Hampshire scene in the final ten or so years of steam operation. I therefore wish to record my appreciation to all of the photographers who have loaned their splendid slides for publication. Without their co-operation, production of this book would not have been possible. In addition, my thanks are also offered to Terence Barry, David J. Fakes and Graham Mallinson who scrutinised the original manuscript and offered many amendments which, I feel, have greatly improved the end product.

Burgess Hill, March 2000   Michael Welch

BOURNEMOUTH WEST TO SOUTHAMPTON

LSWR M7 Class 0–4–4T No 30254 poses at Bournemouth West Station, presumably whilst carrying out station pilot duties, on 19th September 1963. In the mid-19th century Bournemouth was a hamlet within the parish of Holdenhurst which in 1851 could muster a population of only 1,220! The first railway in the area was the route from Southampton to Dorchester via Wimborne which opened in 1847, and incorporated a branch to Hamworthy. Bournemouth was then reached by omnibus from this station, which remained the principal access until a line was opened from Ringwood to Christchurch in 1862. During the final decades of the 19th century Bournemouth's population increased dramatically, a development which was no doubt stimulated by the building of the Broadstone to Bournemouth line, which opened to Poole on 2nd December 1872 and to Bournemouth West Station on 15th June 1874. The connection from there to (what later became) Bournemouth Central was inaugurated in 1888. In more recent times Bournemouth West Station became a victim of the cutbacks during the 1960s, closing in October 1965. The station site is now largely occupied by a maintenance depot for electric rolling stock used on the Weymouth to Waterloo line, so at least it is still used for railway purposes. *Neville Simms*

In the early days of railway development in the area Bournemouth was initially served from the east by a coach service from Christchurch Station, which opened on 13th November 1862. During the following year an Act of Parliament was obtained for a 3½ mile extension from Christchurch across the heathland to Bournemouth. This was opened on 14th March 1870 to a terminus which was located about a quarter mile to the east of the present Bournemouth Station. The latter dates from 20th July 1885 and was known as 'Bournemouth East' until 1st May 1899, when the more impressive suffix 'Central' was bestowed on the station. Bournemouth Central has an impressive facade on the down side, and is one of the few stations in southern England to boast an overall roof. The station originally possessed four through tracks and has two through platforms. In 1928 the down platform was lengthened so that two twelve-coach trains could be accommodated. In this August 1966 view, which was taken from the down platform, Bulleid 'Battle of Britain' Pacific No 34060 *25 Squadron* is depicted hauling empty coaching stock through the station. *Ian Wright*

Hinton Admiral's brightly painted signal box dominates this scene which depicts Bulleid Light Pacific No 34102 *Lapford* passing through the station with an unidentified northbound express on 18th September 1962. The first vehicle of the train is in maroon livery, which may indicate that it was an inter-regional service, perhaps heading for the Midlands or North of England. Note the signalman standing at the open window. Until the 1950s Hinton Admiral Station was surrounded by heathland and woodland, but has now largely been swallowed up by Highcliffe's sprawling residential development. The coast is just over a mile away at this point. No 34102 was destined to have a charmed life, because it survived to become the last active unmodified Bulleid Pacific. Its last recorded passenger working was on 5th July 1967, when it powered the 6.49am Salisbury to Waterloo train. It then worked a van train from London to Basingstoke before retiring to Eastleigh shed to await its last journey to the scrapheap. *Alan Jarvis*

The 'Bournemouth Belle' is one of the most famous, perhaps *the* most famous, trains to serve Hampshire. In this illustration the down 'Belle' is seen in an appealing setting on the fringe of the New Forest, between Brockenhurst and Sway on 19th September 1966. The course of the Lymington branch – which was still steam worked at that time – is just discernible in the background. Motive power was provided by Bulleid 'Merchant Navy' Pacific No 35026 *Lamport & Holt Line*. In contrast to the immaculately presented Pullman Cars, the locomotive is in rather dirty condition, which was a regrettably common feature during the run down of steam traction on the Southern Region. At least No 35026 is still carrying a nameplate on the side of the engine that is visible, but no headboard. No 35026, which was constructed in December 1948 and rebuilt in January 1957, lasted in traffic until March 1967. The opulent and luxurious 'Bournemouth Belle' was introduced in July 1931 and initially ran on every Sunday throughout the year and daily during the summer period. All-year-round daily operation commenced in January 1936, motive power usually being a 'Lord Nelson' 4-6-0. The train did not run during the Second World War, but soon reappeared after the end of hostilities, usually with Bulleid 'Merchant Navy' Pacifics in charge. In January 1967 Brush Type 4 diesels were rostered, but steam frequently deputised and, indeed, the 'Belle' was steam hauled during its last week of operation in July 1967. *Neville Simms*

Lamport & Holt Line is seen again, but this time on 8th October 1966, a few weeks after the previous picture was taken. In this striking, panned action shot it is depicted near Brockenhurst, once again at the head of the 'Bournemouth Belle'. Note the silhouette of the driver who is caught in a classic pose, through the open cab window. *Neville Simms*

An LSWR T9 Class 4–4–0, No 30289, which is in commendably clean condition, pauses between shunting duties at Brockenhurst goods yard on 28th June 1957. The locomotive was working a Bevois Park (Southampton) to Lymington freight train. In the author's view the T9s were one of the classic pre-grouping designs. Sixty-six of these elegant machines were constructed between 1899 and 1901, to the design of Dugald Drummond, and were built at Nine Elms and by Dubs & Co. of Glasgow. Two batches were constructed, the first fifty-one engines having narrower cabs and splashers (as seen here) than the second batch, which possessed full-width splashers in order to accommodate both the driving wheels and the coupling rods. Between 1922 and 1929 the entire class was rebuilt with superheaters and extended smokeboxes, modifications which greatly improved its performance. The last representatives of the class in ordinary service finished work in Cornwall in 1961, but one member (No 30120) was scheduled for preservation as part of the National Collection and can (at the time of writing) be seen on the Bluebell Railway, though it is not currently operational. *R.C. Riley*

The distinctive and outstanding landscape of the New Forest is undoubtedly one of the highlights of a journey along the Bournemouth Line. In this view an unidentified Bournemouth to Waterloo semi-fast train is depicted passing Haseley Inclosure, which is one of the most remote and inaccessible parts of the forest, and located half-way between Brockenhurst and Beaulieu Road stations. What a pity there is not a small herd of ponies visible in the field on the right of the picture to really complete the scene! Motive power is provided by Bulleid 'West Country' Class locomotive No 34004 *Yeovil* and this shot was taken on 1st April 1967. *J. Spencer Gilks*

Another picture taken deep in the heart of the New Forest shows Bulleid Rebuilt Light Pacific No 34036 *Westward Ho!* approaching Beaulieu Road Station with (what appears to be) the 4.23pm boat train from Weymouth to Waterloo on 29th May 1967. The train is formed of a selection of Bulleid and BR Standard coaches, some of the latter being in blue and grey livery. The Weymouth boat trains were noteworthy because they passed through the streets of the town between the main station and the quay. In steam days this location was a well known photographic spot that offered a superb vista across the heathland to the woods beyond, but a visitor today is likely to find that during the intervening years much lineside vegetation has sprung up, ruining the scene for railway photographers. Like most members of its class, No 34036 was built at Brighton Works, emerging in July 1946. It was rebuilt in September 1960 and remained in service until SR steam traction came to an end in July 1967. One of the highlights of its career occurred on 5th July 1967 when it powered the last steam-hauled 'Bournemouth Belle' from Bournemouth to Waterloo. *David Clark*

In this pleasing view, a BR Standard Class 4MT 2–6–4T, No 80082, is pictured passing Millbrook Station, in the Southampton suburbs, with an unidentified down working on 20th March 1966. The unusual siting of this island platform station, which is located between the up and down slow lines, is of interest. The coach immediately behind the locomotive is an early BR Mark II First Class corridor vehicle, an 'FK' in railwaymen's parlance, which was almost brand new at the time of the photograph – hence its smart appearance. This vehicle was one of the few Mark II carriages equipped with vacuum brakes and steam heating (to facilitate steam haulage) before a change of policy was made in favour of air braked and electrically heated vehicles, for use with modern traction. The remainder of the coaches are of BR Standard Mark I or Bulleid design. Note the attractive backdrop to this illustration, particularly the Victorian villas and elegant church spire. Alas, a similar picture taken today would be dominated by an urban motorway flyover, most of the houses having been sacrificed in the name of 'progress', although the church has mercifully survived the onslaught. *Roy Hobbs*

SOUTHAMPTON DOCKS

In this very rare, possibly unique, colour illustration Southern Region USA Class 0–6–0T locomotive No s73 is depicted shunting at Southampton Docks in 1949. The engine is displaying its Southern Railway number with a temporary 's' prefix, this being a short lived identification system which was only used briefly during the very early days of the BR regime to denote the region to which an engine was allocated. In addition, and rather incongruously, the 'British Railways' legend on the tankside is in Southern Railway 'Sunshine' lettering. Presumably Eastleigh Works was still using the old transfers until the new BR stocks arrived! Only two of the fourteen members of this class are known to have carried the temporary 's' prefix, so this shot is of considerable historical significance. Loco s73 was built by Vulcan Ironworks in the United States in 1943, shipped to Great Britain, and became War Department No 1974. Following purchase by the Southern Railway, it started work in the docks in June 1947 and in March 1948 underwent modifications at Eastleigh Works, which included improved cab ventilation and an enlarged coal bunker. It later became one of only four USA tanks engines to carry malachite green colours and is depicted looking very smart in this livery elsewhere in this album. *S.C. Townroe/Colour-Rail*

The USA tank locomotives were an everyday sight in the docks area at Southampton for more than fifteen years, and in this picture a rather decrepit looking No 30069 is seen shunting on 26th April 1962. During 1962 diesel shunters largely displaced the 'Yankee Tanks', as they were known colloquially, but some members of the class were transferred to departmental service, while others were moved from Southampton Docks shed to Eastleigh, being specially retained to work banana trains, which required to be steam heated at the docks during the winter months. No 30069 was one of these engines, and despite having lost its principal duties, it managed to survive in traffic until the end of steam on the SR in July 1967, when it was despatched to a large dump of condemned locomotives which had congregated at the former Salisbury shed. No 30069 was one of five USA Class tank engines at the dump, and two of these were subsequently rescued for preservation. Unfortunately, No 30069 was not one of those selected, and was later scrapped at Cashmore's scrap yard at Newport in South Wales. *Colin Hogg*

In the mid-1960s the SR still handled substantial boat train traffic to and from Southampton and the world famous Cunard liners still plied the Atlantic. The *Queen Mary* and *Queen Elizabeth* represented the finest standards in luxury and service, their passengers no doubt being considerably pampered during the Atlantic crossing. After all, the shipping companies were losing out to the airlines and although they could never compete on speed, at least they were able to make a voyage an experience to remember. The SR provided connecting boat trains – sometimes with special headboards – for the exclusive use of London passengers. These employed special sets of rolling stock, and ran to the Ocean Liner Terminal at Southampton. Alas, the prestigious nature of the operation does not seem to have filtered down to the motive power department which, at least towards the end of steam, turned out any express passenger locomotive for these trains, regardless of its mechanical state or external condition. On 31st August 1965 the *Queen Elizabeth* arrived at Southampton, presumably from New York, and Bulleid Pacific No 34088 *213 Squadron*, in absolutely disgraceful external condition, was rostered to haul one of the boat trains to the Capital, and is seen outside the Ocean Liner Terminal building. One shudders to think what well-heeled American visitors thought when this filthy machine backed down on to their train. It could hardly have made a very favourable first impression! *Neville Simms*

SOUTHAMPTON TO BASINGSTOKE

Undoubtedly one of the most popular photographic locations in Hampshire was the west end of Southampton Central Station, where there was a magnificent signal gantry just beyond the end of the down platforms. An oasis of semaphore signalling, including the gantry seen here, survived at Southampton until the early 1980s, when it was replaced by the all-conquering colour light signals. In this superb study 'Merchant Navy' Pacific No 35030 *Elder Dempster Lines* is pictured apparently making a quick getaway with the 10.30am from Waterloo to Weymouth on 5th November 1966. The SR operating authorities were doing their best to reduce the number of steam turns as quickly as possible at this time, using diesel-hauled 3TC/4TC units (the Bournemouth Line replacement stock), plus a small fleet of Brush Type 4 diesel locomotives which were given derogatory nicknames by the steam fans. By January 1967 many of the most arduous steam diagrams had been taken over by diesels, at least in theory! In reality, many of the diesel replacements were even more unreliable than the steam engines they were intended to replace and, much to the delight of the enthusiast fraternity, steam substitutions abounded. On 9th July 1967 *Elder Dempster Lines* earned its place in the history books when it powered the 2.11pm Weymouth to Waterloo train, the very last ordinary steam-hauled passenger train to run in Hampshire. *Neville Simms*

During the mid-1960s Western Region 'Hall' Class 4–6–0s were a regular sight in Hampshire powering the Poole to York (and vice versa) trains, which they worked between Oxford and Poole. In October 1965 the engine workings were revised, a Banbury-based LMSR Class 5MT 4–6–0 being rostered. The engines worked the down train on one day and returned from Poole the following day. On 3rd January 1966, Class 5MT No 45198 was photographed awaiting departure from Southampton with the northbound working. These trains gave observers a welcome break from the monotonous power which characterised the South Western Division during the last years of steam. It is recorded that no fewer than 35 different 'Black Fives' appeared on these workings during 1966, the most common examples being Nos 44942 and 45493, both of which were kept in reasonably clean condition. These trains were routed via the Great Central main line, and when this line was closed as a through route in September 1966 the locomotive diagrams were, once again, altered with diesel haulage being employed north of Basingstoke and a Bulleid Pacific being used on the SR. Southampton Central Station's clock tower, which dominates the background, was a well-known landmark in the city, but was regrettably demolished when the up side of the station was rebuilt in the mid-1960s. *The late Derek Cross*

This viewpoint, looking westwards from Southampton Central's down main line platform with
the station's signal gantry prominent, must have been photographed many times during the
closing years of steam. Here, in time-honoured fashion, the driver of No 35008, *Orient Line*,
checks the locomotive's bearings for possible overheating. The 'Merchant Navy' Class Pacific was
powering an unidentified Waterloo to Weymouth train on 3rd January 1966. *Orient Line* was
active right up to the bitter end of SR steam, and was selected to work an official 9.55am
Waterloo to Weymouth 'Farewell to Steam' special on 2nd July 1967. No 35028 *Clan Line* hauled
a Waterloo to Bournemouth 'Farewell' special on the same day. Many enthusiasts shunned these
trains due to the high fare being demanded, and also the fact that the regular 9.33am Waterloo to
Bournemouth summer excursion train was also running and offered steam haulage on a normal
service train. However, the participants on 35008's run enjoyed excellent value for money, with
maximum speeds of 88mph and 90mph being obtained on the down and up runs respectively.
The late Derek Cross

14

In the author's opinion the sound and smell of a steam
locomotive are qualities that are just as attractive as the sight
of one. At night-time these sensations are heightened, and
perhaps one of the most memorable experiences during the age
of steam was the distant, haunting whistle of a locomotive lost
somewhere in the darkness. Unfortunately, few railway
photographers experimented with time exposure shots which
could capture the indefinable magic of the steam railway after
dark. But here is a picture which brilliantly portrays the special
atmosphere of steam traction at night. The location is the east
end of Southampton Central Station and this dramatic view of
No 35026 *Lamport & Holt Line* was recorded in February 1966.
L.F. Folkard/Colour-Rail

A view of Southampton Terminus Station on 26th June 1957, showing a very smartly presented BR Standard Class 4MT No 76064 at the head of a train of Maunsell stock in crimson and cream livery. No 76064 was less than a year old when this shot was taken. Southampton Terminus was the city's first passenger station, services to Winchester beginning on 10th June 1839. Trains to and from London commenced on 11th May 1840, following completion of the Winchester to Basingstoke section of the LSWR's main line. The station had six curved platforms, and also possessed a substantial signal box which, rather curiously, was called 'Southampton Yard' and not named after the station it served. The massive building in the background is the hotel erected by the LSWR principally for use by their maritime passengers, but was later employed as offices by the Cunard shipping line. Perhaps the most interesting feature of the station was the considerable number of visiting *ex*-GWR locomotives which powered cross-country trains to Cheltenham and Didcot, until these routes were shut in the early 1960s. Southampton Terminus Station was closed to passengers on 5th September 1966, but temporarily reopened for parcels traffic until March 1968. The site is now a car park, but the elegant main station building has been preserved and has latterly been used as a restaurant. *R.C. Riley*

In this remarkably 'busy' scene – there are at least four engines at work within camera range – a Maunsell 'Lord Nelson' Class 4–6–0 No 30857 *Lord Howe* is depicted approaching Southampton Terminus on 26th June 1957. The locomotive was working a boat train carrying Greek Line passengers from Waterloo, and was travelling on the down main line which by-passed the station and headed directly across Canute Road and into the docks. A rake of vintage LSWR coaches, on the left of the picture, adds colour to the scene. The freight train on the right of the picture is standing on the goods only lines which were installed by the LSWR to relieve congestion at the approach to the docks. Following the station's closure, and the decline of rail traffic into the docks, the layout in this area was severely rationalised and, almost unbelievably, only a single track now remains. *R.C. Riley*

BR Standard Class 4MT No 76064 passes St Denys Station in charge of a Waterloo to Southampton Docks boat train on 1st July 1967. These moderately powered 2–6–0s would not normally have worked such a heavy train, so the appearance of 76064 may have been the result of a shortage of motive power, or perhaps it replaced a failed locomotive earlier on the journey. The tightly curved tracks diverging to the right in the shot are those of the line to Fareham and Portsmouth. St Denys boasted a fine array of semaphore signals, some of which are visible in the background, but these have long since disappeared. *The late Derek Cross*

The BR footplatemen's strike of 1955 inflicted untold damage on the railway industry, which lost a lot of freight traffic which never returned. In addition, passengers suffered considerable inconvenience and many of them doubtless turned their backs on the railway, also never to return. Nearly all of the locomotive fleet was confined to the engine sheds, so the only beneficiaries of the prolonged dispute appear to have been the train spotters who were no doubt delighted to find sheds packed with engines as never before – that is assuming they could reach them, of course! Scenes like the one here, which shows many rows of stationary engines at Eastleigh shed, must have been the realisation of every train spotter's wildest dream. What a pity the strike situation was more akin to a nightmare for virtually everybody else! *S.C. Townroe/Colour-Rail*

Eastleigh, with its works and sizeable engine shed was, of course, a Mecca for enthusiasts in steam days. One of the principal attractions for steam fans was the fact that obscure locomotives, perhaps from some far-flung corner of the SR, would occasionally turn up at the works for overhaul or, more likely towards the end of steam, cutting-up at the back of the works. Here, two particularly interesting engines, both of which had been withdrawn from service stock during the early 1960s, are pictured at the works on 3rd March 1963. They were departmental service locomotives, which meant that they were not in ordinary traffic, but nominated to work exclusively as shunters at allocated railway engineering depots or works. The engine on the left is LSWR G6 Class 0–6–0T No DS682 (former running No 30272) which was the shunter at Meldon Quarry, near Okehampton, for some years. The other locomotive is a former Lancing Carriage Works shunter, No DS680, a LBSCR 'Terrier' 0–6–0T. This engine was originally built in February 1876 and sold to the SECR in 1904 for use on the Isle of Sheppey Light Railway. It entered service stock at Lancing in December 1932, and was based there until June 1962, when it was presented to the Canadian Railway Historical Association. It was restored at Eastleigh before being shipped to Canada. The G6 was not destined to be so fortunate and was later broken up. The tall building in the background is the diesel depot which was built in connection with the Hampshire dieselisation scheme in about 1957. *Mike Hudson*

A Southern Railway Z Class 0–8–0T locomotive No 30950 undergoes a heavy overhaul in Eastleigh Works on 18th September 1960. At the end of the nineteenth century the LSWR's principal locomotive repair works was at Nine Elms, London, and the company badly needed larger and more efficient premises in order to speed up the repair of its fleet. The LSWR had already moved their carriage and wagon works from London in 1891, and Eastleigh was also selected for the locomotive works. A site situated south-east of the station was chosen, between the line to Portsmouth and the running shed complex, thus creating the largest 'railway town' in the south of England. The staff and equipment were transferred from Nine Elms and the new works opened in 1909. The first engine to be built at the works was S14 Class 0–4–0 motor tank No 101, which was completed in 1910, and between that time and 1950 around 300 engines were constructed at the works, and many more overhauled. Electrification of the Waterloo to Bournemouth line, which was announced in 1964, presaged the end of Eastleigh Works' long association with the steam locomotive. The last one to be repaired there was 'Battle of Britain' Pacific No 34089 *602 Squadron* which was outshopped amidst a blaze of local publicity in October 1966. There were fears that the works would be closed, but it remains operational, albeit on a greatly reduced scale, the glory days of Eastleigh Works having long since passed. *Trevor Owen*

A road bridge south of Eastleigh Station, which gave a clear, uninterrupted view of the main line, was always a favourite haunt of enthusiasts. The road also gave access to the works and shed, so the bridge was often lined with crowds of spotters. Here, Bulleid Light Pacific No 34097 *Holsworthy* is seen speeding towards Southampton with a Waterloo to Bournemouth service on 3rd May 1958. This was one of only six Light Pacifics built at Eastleigh, the remainder being constructed at Brighton. On the right, H15 Class 4–6–0 No 30331 is apparently waiting for the express to pass before crossing on to the up main line. The roofs in the distance, beyond the coaches, are those of the carriage works. *Trevor Owen/Colour-Rail*

Photographed from a high road overbridge south of the station, LSWR M7 Class 0–4–4T No 30376, running bunker first, leaves Winchester City with a down local working on 24th June 1957. The two coaches immediately behind the engine are from the Maunsell era, while the third vehicle is a Bulleid-designed carriage. An unidentified van brings up the rear of the train. Winchester was the northern terminus of the LSWR's line from Southampton, which opened on 10th June 1839. It lost this status when the route to London was opened throughout on 11th May 1840. The name 'Winchester City' was coined by BR in 1949 in order to avoid confusion with the former GWR Chesil station. Despite the closure of the latter in the early 1960s, the suffix 'City' continued to be used until the Bournemouth Line electrification scheme was inaugurated on 10th July 1967. In 1965 the southern connection to the goods yard, on the left, was removed to permit an extension of the up platform. *R.C. Riley*

Winchester was known for its cramped goods yard, which had sharply curved tracks. Shunting in the yard was restricted to the short wheelbase LSWR B4 Class 0–4–0Ts, which had their own corrugated iron-clad shed, visible in the background, which was erected in 1928. The shunter usually spent the week at Winchester and returned to Eastleigh shed at weekends. Occasionally, when a B4 was not available, a SECR P Class 0–6–0T was substituted, and in this rare picture No 31325 is seen taking a break between shunting activities on 24th June 1957. An up train headed by BR Standard Class 4MT No 76067 appears to be pulling out of the station. Note the old signal box, which was replaced in 1960, and the vintage Morris Commercial Post Office van, which is almost hidden on the extreme left of the picture. *R.C. Riley*

North of Winchester the railway traverses a very sparsely populated area of Hampshire, which lies on a rather featureless chalk plain. Apart from Winchester Junction, where the line to Alton diverged, the first major point of interest is Wallers Ash Tunnel (501 yds). The tunnel is just discernible in the background of this shot of Bulleid Pacific No 35003 *Royal Mail* hauling a Bournemouth to Waterloo express on 12th July 1965. Out of view, behind the photographer, is the start of a 1¼ mile long quadruple track section, known as the 'Wallers Ash Loops', after the signal box of that name which was located at the southern end. Slow moving freight trains could be diverted into the loop lines, thus enabling fast passenger trains to overtake. The northern end of the loops was controlled by Weston signal box. The line climbs all of the way from St Denys to Litchfield Tunnel – a distance of more than twenty miles – on a ruling gradient of 1 in 252, so this stretch caused a lot of hard work for firemen! *Paul Leavens*

Rebuilt Bulleid Pacific No 34040 *Crewkerne*, complete with its nameplates and in quite clean condition, makes a fine sight in the evening sunshine as it heads south from Micheldever. No 34040, hauling a block train of cement wagons, was photographed at 7.50pm on 18th June 1966. *David Clark*

The isolated, rural station of Micheldever is the only one on the 18¾ miles section between Winchester and Basingstoke. The village of Micheldever is located about three miles to the south. When the station opened it was known as 'Andover Road', being the nearest station to that town, but its name was altered in 1856 when Andover gained its own station. The interesting station building, on the left, was constructed of local flint with yellow brick quoins (cornerstones), and is one of the most attractive in Hampshire. The immediate environs of the station are dominated by a former chalk quarry, which was excavated by the LSWR, and chalk continued to be removed by the SR. During the 1930s 5,000 tons were reportedly being taken away each week in connection with the construction of new docks at Southampton. The quarry site was later used for the storage of rolling stock and, more recently, has been used as an oil terminal. The line through Micheldever was quadrupled around the turn of the century and an island platform installed, upon which the signal box was located. Later the island platform fell into disuse and became overgrown. In April 1966 the outside pair of tracks was taken out of use however, and the island platform was refurbished and restored to regular use. In this illustration No 34108 *Wincanton*, which had unfortunately lost its front number plate, speeds downhill through the station with a train of assorted vans on 6th June 1967. *David Clark*

A truly evocative scene as Bulleid Pacific No 34102 *Lapford*, crosses Battledown flyover with an up Bournemouth train on 27th October 1962. Note how the Pacific's pure white exhaust is hanging in the still air of what appears to have been a glorious autumn morning. The tracks passing beneath are those of the Salisbury Line. The flyover at Battledown, and the quadruple track section onwards to Basingstoke, came into operation on 30th May 1897, some years before the Basingstoke to Woking section was quadrupled. *Trevor Owen*

The Bournemouth Line has always been a predominantly passenger route, conveying heavy holiday and excursion traffic, and most of the freight working was to and from Southampton Docks. Here, Maunsell S15 Class 4–6–0 No 30825, in quite clean condition, is seen near Worting Junction with a southbound freight in tow in September 1960. Judging by the headcode disc it was heading for Southampton Docks. Locomotives of this class were built in various batches from 1920 to 1938, the earlier engines being designed by Urie. The later engines were designed by Maunsell, who made many alterations to the original specification, including higher boiler pressure and modified cabs. *Paul Leavens*

A scene at Basingstoke Station on 21st July 1962 showing S15 Class No 30498 posing in the slow line platform with what is presumably a semi-fast train to Waterloo. The two coaches formed immediately behind the locomotive are both Maunsell-designed Open Third vehicles dating from the mid-1930s. The first railway to reach Basingstoke opened from Winchfield (then called Shapley Heath) on 10th June 1839. On 11th May 1840 the section onwards to Winchester was completed and through running between London and Southampton started. The 13½-mile long line to Reading was built by the GWR and was opened to the GWR's station, which was adjacent to the LSWR's premises, on 1st November 1848. It was originally broad gauge, but the GWR was instructed by Parliament to convert the line to dual gauge operation, the first standard gauge train arriving at Basingstoke from Reading on 22nd December 1856. The broad gauge was removed from the line in 1869, and the GWR's separate station was closed in January 1932, its trains thereafter using the SR's platforms. *Neville Simms*

During the run-down of SR steam, official policy was to keep the fleet running at minimum cost and as a result many engines finished their careers in parlous condition. But at least the SR's fleet did not quite sink to the absolutely disgraceful state that many WR locomotives were in during their final year. Apart from usually being indescribably filthy, the engines were often running bereft of name and numberplates, a crudely painted number on the smokebox door sometimes being the only method of identification. Some locomotives even ran around minus their safety valve bonnets. What had happened to that old Great Western pride? The condition of 'Hall' Class 4–6–0 No 7924 *Thornycroft Hall*, which was working a Bournemouth to Newcastle train on 31st July 1965, does not appear to be too decrepit by the appalling WR standards of the day, and indeed the engine lasted until WR steam breathed its last at the end of 1965. WR power was ousted from this inter-regional working in October 1965, when LMSR 'Black Fives' took over. *Paul Leavens*

Much of the London & Southampton Railway's route was brilliantly engineered by Joseph Locke, an eminent railway engineer of the day, who was appointed by the company in 1837. The route is very much a high speed line with no severe curves, apart from one just outside Southampton, and no gradient greater than 1 in 250. Maunsell 'King Arthur' Class 4–6–0 No 30796 *Sir Dodinas le Savage* accelerates away from Basingstoke with the 8.46am Salisbury to Waterloo train on the bright morning of 9th September 1961. By this date the 'King Arthurs' were in their twilight years and at the time of this picture only thirteen remained operational. At least the class had a good innings. No 30796, for example, was built at Eastleigh Works in May 1926 and lasted in service for a further five months after this scene was recorded. In the late 1920s it sometimes powered the 'Southern Belle' Pullman Car train between Victoria and Brighton. *Paul Leavens*

BASINGSTOKE TO FARNBOROUGH

The LBSCR K Class 'Moguls' were mostly based in Sussex and rarely strayed far from their home sheds, apart from visits to London on freight duty or seasonal passenger workings. So this illustration of No 32345 leaving Basingstoke on 8th September 1962 at the head of a train of passenger stock is something of a mystery. Perhaps the date holds a clue to the identity of the working. The Farnborough Air Display took place on that day, so it is probable that 32345 had been commandeered from the Central Section to haul an additional passenger train from Farnborough to Waterloo, and the working seen here is actually an empty stock movement proceeding to Farnborough. Sadly, this may have been No 32345's final appearance at the head of a passenger train, because these lovely 'Brighton' engines were all withdrawn three months later. *Neville Simms*

An S15 Class 4–6–0, No 30826, runs into Winchfield with an afternoon Basingstoke to Waterloo semi-fast train on 1st September 1962. The platform on the left was originally the down platform, which became largely disused when the line was quadrupled by the LSWR in 1904. Its grassy surface has apparently been maintained in a reasonable condition in case it was required for use in an emergency. *Neville Simms*

In this panoramic view of Winchfield Station, Maunsell 'Schools' Class 4–4–0 No 30921 *Shrewsbury* is seen leaving in charge of a Waterloo to Basingstoke semi-fast train on 1st September 1962. For a brief period, from 24th September 1838 until 10th June 1839, Winchfield – which was then known as Shapley Heath – was the 'end of the line' for services from London. The section between Basingstoke and Brookwood was famous for its air-operated lower quadrant signals, which were installed by the LSWR at the turn of the century. The signals seen here, however, are of the orthodox upper quadrant type, so presumably the original signals had become worn out and were replaced at some stage. Note that the signalman has already replaced the signal arm to danger. The 'Schools' were designed for the Hastings Line, but a small number operated on the Western Section almost from the day they were built. When the Hastings Line was dieselised in the late 1950s the 'Schools' were displaced, and the class again became common on the South Western Section. *Neville Simms*

Bulleid Light Pacific No 34052 *Lord Dowding* is seen near Farnborough on 5th August 1965 hauling a morning commuter train to London, which had presumably originated at Basingstoke. A few London commuter services, notably the 7.50am Basingstoke to Waterloo and 5.09pm return, remained steam worked until almost the end of SR steam, a Bulleid Pacific being normally rostered for these workings. These trains could be recognised immediately because their formations normally included BR Standard non-corridor vehicles, which provided extra seating capacity. Judging by the new ballast, the fast tracks at this location had been relaid just before this picture was taken. During the ensuing eighteen months much of the Bournemouth Line was relaid in preparation for electrification and scenes such as this became common up and down the line. Unfortunately this essential work, combined with poor performances from the increasingly neglected steam locomotive fleet, had a disastrous effect on punctuality, particularly during the latter half of 1966. This resulted in bitter complaints being made to BR by Hampshire Members of Parliament, and the press being inundated with letters from disgruntled travellers. In a desperate attempt to improve the situation, the SR acquired six Brush Type 4 diesels, but alas they proved to be just as unreliable as the steam engines they were intended to replace. *Trevor Owen*

A brilliant Christmas card scene at Farnborough on 1st January 1962 as an
unidentified BR Standard Class 5MT leaves with a semi-fast train to Waterloo. The
heavy snowfall actually occurred during the previous day, with the result that most
services on the routes from Hampshire to London were brought to an almost complete
standstill, with Waterloo Station being closed for several hours during the evening
rush hour period. The up 'Atlantic Coast Express' was one of the trains affected by
the severe weather, and reportedly terminated at Clapham Junction! By the following
morning services had been restored on all lines, but these were not running to a
normal timetable and those trains that did operate were often short of their usual
number of coaches. *Trevor Owen*

The same view as that in the previous picture is depicted in normal weather conditions and shows Bulleid 'West Country' Class Pacific No 34037 *Clovelly* pulling away from Farnborough with an up local working on 22nd September 1962. The four coach train, plus a van, hardly constituted a demanding assignment for such a powerful locomotive. Like nearly all of its sister engines, No 34037 was a product of Brighton Works, emerging in August 1946. In March 1958 it was rebuilt and survived in traffic until the cessation of steam traction on the SR from 10th July 1967. On the penultimate day of SR steam *Clovelly* was very busy, powering the 2.30am Waterloo to Portsmouth newspaper train before hauling the 11.26am Portsmouth Harbour to Colne holiday extra as far as Mitre Bridge Junction. Later it worked the 6.20pm additional boat train from Waterloo to Southampton Docks, reputedly the final daylight scheduled steam departure from Waterloo. *Alan Jarvis*

A rare colour picture of Ringwood Station taken on 3rd September 1963, with a BR Standard 'Mogul' waiting in the platform at the head of an eastbound van train. The most interesting feature of Ringwood Station was the train shed on the left which was used by Christchurch branch services until they were withdrawn in 1935. Much of the area seen here has since been obliterated by housing development. *David Wigley*

RINGWOOD TO BROCKENHURST

A view of Holmsley Station taken shortly before closure, looking towards Brockenhurst. Note the dropped platform edge on the up side, which must have presented quite a challenge to elderly passengers. Only a small number of people used the station however, there being no settlement within reasonable distance. The roadbridge carried the A35 Southampton to Christchurch road across the railway and an access road to it now occupies the course of the railway at this point. Despite the proliferation of roads the station house is still *in situ* and is now a tea room. From its opening in 1847 until November 1862 the station was known as 'Christchurch Road', that town being about seven miles distant. *Gerald Daniels*

The 60½-mile long line between Southampton and Dorchester was opened on 1st June 1847. The single track wound among the low hills and heathlands of this area in order to serve places such as Ringwood and Wimborne which, at that time, were of much more importance than Bournemouth. When the line opened the latter place was little more than a hamlet consisting of a coastguard station and around thirty houses! The Southampton and Dorchester Railway was promoted under the energetic leadership of Mr A.L. Castleman, a Wimborne solicitor, and the line became known as 'Castleman's Corkscrew' due to its sinuous route. It should be noted, however, that most of the route in Hampshire became part of the Bournemouth Line, leaving only a relatively short stretch – between Ringwood and Brockenhurst – to be covered in this section of the album. The latter line suffered a reduction in status largely as a result of the rapid growth of Bournemouth. It had begun life as the sole route in the area, but ultimately became a tranquil backwater with a meagre service of around half a dozen trains a day in each direction and even these ceased to operate when the line succumbed to closure in May 1964. It is a pity that BR made little attempt to economise on many of its country routes, and here unmodified Bulleid Pacific No 34103 *Calstock* is seen leaving Holmsley on 18th September 1962 with a short train heading towards Brockenhurst. It was possible, however, that No 34103 was being returned to its home shed – hence its use on such a short train in order to save a light engine working. *Alan Jarvis*

WIMBORNE TO SALISBURY

The 28¼-mile long Salisbury to Wimborne line, promoted by the Salisbury & Dorset Junction Company, was incorporated in 1861. The opening date for the single line route was 20th December 1866. The line passed through three counties – Wiltshire, Hampshire and Dorset – but only a comparatively short section was in Hampshire, and therefore within the scope of this book. The line traversed a sparsely inhabited area and only had a service of around half a dozen weekday trains a day, even when traffic was at its heaviest prior to World War Two. On summer Saturdays in the 1950s the route was used by holiday trains from South Wales to Bournemouth. Closure occurred in 1964 and the railway authorities lost no time in lifting the track of this little known line, which never really prospered at any time during its career. The line is unlikely to have been photographed widely in colour (or black and white!), so this is probably one of the few colour shots of the line in existence. In this melancholy view, a demolition train pauses at Breamore on 19th August 1965, with BR Standard Class 4MT No 76007 in charge. *David Wigley*

THE LYMINGTON BRANCH

The branch from Lymington Junction, near Brockenhurst, to the small port of Lymington was opened by the Lymington Railway Company on 12th July 1858. The port was the terminus of ferry services from the Isle of Wight and the company hoped to develop traffic, but the LSWR concentrated on the Portsmouth to Ryde route and as a result the Lymington branch did not initially attract the custom anticipated. After the LSWR had absorbed the independent Lymington company in 1878 the former began to take more interest in the branch, and an extension from Lymington Town to the pier was opened on 1st May 1884, the ferries also being taken over by the LSWR in the same year. In 1938 the SR introduced one of the first 'drive on, drive off' ferry services at Lymington. Curiously, the branch has always been associated with unadvertised private halts, the first being opened at Shirley Holms around 1860; it remained in use until about 1888. The best known of the halts is Ampress Works, which was commissioned on 1st October 1956 to serve Messrs Wellworthy's factory. In this appealing view LSWR M7 Class 0–4–4T No 30053 is seen approaching Lymington Town from the Pier Station with a Brockenhurst-bound working on 16th May 1964. The branch was the last refuge for the ageing M7s and by the time of this picture the survivors were completely worn out. Doubtless much to the relief of the engine crews, they were replaced by more modern locomotives during the following month. No 30053 was later preserved and in 1967 was shipped to the Steamtown Railway Museum in Vermont, USA – surely the longest journey an M7 ever made! In 1987 it was rescued by the 'Southern Repatriation Group' and can today be seen on the Purbeck line at Swanage, Dorset, thus returning the engine to one of its former haunts. *Roy Hobbs*

A portrait of Lymington Pier Station in July 1957, showing M7 Class No 30028 awaiting departure with a train to Brockenhurst. In 1938 a slipway was constructed to enable end-loading vehicle ferries to be introduced. At the same time the platform canopy was reconstructed, with a wall in order to reduce draughts, and the level crossing installed to provide access to the slipway. Through trains to and from Waterloo used to run to Lymington Pier during the summer months, and latterly these sometimes employed 'Schools' Class 4–4–0s as far as Brockenhurst, where a Maunsell Q Class 0–6–0 normally took over for the short trip down the branch. *John Edgington*

Running around the train was always a tricky business for enginemen at Lymington Pier and really required drivers with a particularly delicate touch. The reason for this is clearly apparent in this photograph – one false move and you could finish up 'parking' your locomotive in the Lymington River! In this picture BR Standard Class 4MT No 80152 is seen running round at the south end of the station in early 1967. Following the demise of the M7s in 1964, these engines became a common sight on the line, sharing the duties with LMSR-designed Ivatt 2–6–2Ts. The Lymington line later became famous as Great Britain's last steam-worked passenger branch. Diesel-electric units displaced steam traction from 3rd April 1967, but they were only a stopgap measure until electrification in July of the same year. A misty, distant outline of the Isle of Wight is just discernible in the background. *John Phillips*

SALISBURY TO BASINGSTOKE

Without a doubt the best-known train that traversed this route was the 'Atlantic Coast Express' which is seen here passing Grateley behind No 35018 *British India Line* on 16th September 1958. The 'Atlantic Coast Express', or 'ACE' as it was commonly known, first ran in 1928, but the ancestry of the train can be traced back to the 1890s when the LSWR first ran an 11.00am express from Waterloo to the West Country. The 'ACE' became the most multi-portioned train in Great Britain, one of its distinguishing features being the preponderance of brake composite coaches which were essential for the various portions serving holiday resorts in Devon and Cornwall. In 1952 some services on the SR were substantially accelerated and these changes involved the 'Atlantic Coast Express' which was given the SR's first mile-a-minute schedule. By 1961 the 'ACE' was booked to run the 83¾ miles between Waterloo and Salisbury in 80 minutes. In 1963 some regional boundary changes occurred and the WR took control of the route west of Salisbury, with the inevitable result that the 'ACE' ran for the last time in September 1964. Grateley was the junction for the short branch to Bulford, hence the junction signal at the end of the platform. Note the wind pump on the right of the shot, behind the station building. The first section of this route, then single track, was opened from Basingstoke to Andover on 3rd July 1854. The line was completed through to Salisbury in May 1857.
Trevor Owen

A general view of the west end of Andover Junction Station on 6th June 1967. In the foreground Bulleid Pacific No 34095 *Brentor*, which had just arrived on the 4.51pm Basingstoke to Salisbury stopping train, shunts a parcels van prior to resuming its westbound journey. The 4.51pm was one of a number of steam passenger workings which still served Salisbury, even at this late stage in the run-down of SR steam traction. At this time there were apparently four down trains booked for steam, but only three up workings, so presumably there must have been an up van or freight train booked for steam. *David Clark*

An unidentified down train, with Bulleid 'West Country' Pacific No 34100 *Appledore* in charge, waits in the platform at Andover on 15th May 1965. In the early 1960s No 34100 was based at Stewarts Lane shed where it was kept looking very smart, in sad contrast to its neglected condition in this picture. *Appledore* was used on boat train duties, which included working the famous 'Golden Arrow' from Victoria to Dover, and on 11th June 1961 it hauled the final workings of that train when steam traction bowed out on the Eastern Section. No 34100 remained in service on the South Western Section until SR steam finished in July 1967. *David Wigley*

Rebuilt 'Merchant Navy' Pacific No 35009 *Shaw Savill*, in superb external condition, pauses at Andover Junction while working an Exeter to Waterloo express in July 1957. The uniform green livery of the coaching stock is broken by a single carriage in carmine and cream colours which is formed in the middle of the train. No 35009 was constructed in June 1942 and rebuilt at Eastleigh Works in March 1957, only four months prior to this picture being taken. It was one of the first of the class to be condemned, an event which occurred in July 1964 following a decision to cease heavy repairs on the class. *John Edgington*

Rebuilt 'Merchant Navy' Pacific No 35023 *Holland-Afrika Line* races across Hurstbourne Viaduct with the Locomotive Club of Great Britain's 'Hampshire Branch Lines' rail tour on 9th April 1967. At this time, which was only three months before the extinction of SR steam, there seemed to be a rail tour running every weekend in Hampshire, and occasionally there were two on the same day! This tour later took participants along the Fawley and Lymington branches, but perhaps the most amazing thing about this train was the incredible variety of motive power used during the day, which totalled ten different engines from eight separate classes. *J. Spencer Gilks*

In this rarely photographed scene a BR Standard Class 4MT tank locomotive, No 80152, is depicted shunting at Overton paper mill on 5th July 1967. This picture was taken during the very last week of SR steam and this may have been the final occasion on which steam power was employed on this duty, because most freight workings were rostered for diesel traction by this time. Perhaps they may not know it, but virtually every citizen in the land has a tenuous association with the mill, because it produces the paper on which English banknotes are printed. No 80152 led an unremarkable life, though it did appear on a rail tour on 17th September 1966 when it hauled a London Victoria to Salisbury via Brighton special, from Eastleigh to Salisbury and return. On 8th July 1967, the penultimate day of SR steam, 80152 detached a couple of carriages from the 8.35am Waterloo to Weymouth train at Southampton Central and took them around to the Eastern Docks, very likely the last time a steam engine undertook such a movement. *David Wigley*

Neatly framed by the station footbridge, a dirty Bulleid Pacific No 34032 *Camelford*, pauses at Overton while working an up stopping train on 7th June 1965. The coaches formed immediately behind the engine are BR Standard vehicles. No 34032 first saw the light of day as Southern Railway No 21C132 at Brighton Works in June 1946. Like all of Bulleid's Pacifics, it was originally fitted with air-smoothed casing, but this was discarded when *Camelford* was rebuilt in October 1960. No 34032 did not quite survive until the end of steam, being withdrawn from service in October 1966. *David Clark*

The last station before Worting Junction was Oakley, which was situated about five miles from the centre of Basingstoke. It was a typical LSWR wayside station but, perhaps because the local bus was more convenient for people travelling to Basingstoke, it became a closure casualty on 17th June 1963, before the Beeching Plan started to be implemented. This picture was taken on 15th May 1965, almost two years after the station's closure, but the buildings remain intact, if a trifle weatherbeaten. Note that the signal box is still very much in use despite the closure of the station. *David Wigley*

The route from Basingstoke to Salisbury diverges from the Bournemouth Line at Worting Junction and crosses the county border into Wiltshire between Grateley and the former Porton Station. In 1963 administration of the route was partially transferred to the Western Region and its downgrading to secondary status quickly followed as part of the rationalisation of routes under the Beeching Plan. On 7th September 1964 the WR introduced a semi-fast diesel hauled service between London and Exeter St Davids only, and all through carriages to places beyond Exeter were withdrawn. Regular steam passenger working west of Salisbury was banished from the same date. In this view a splendidly clean Bulleid 'Merchant Navy' Class Pacific No 35014 *Nederland Line* is seen galloping along near Worting Junction at the head of an express from Waterloo to the West of England on 27th October 1962. *Trevor Owen*

THE FAWLEY BRANCH

The history of the Fawley branch can be traced back to 1903 when the LSWR obtained a Light Railway Order to construct a line from Totton to Fawley, down the western shore of Southampton Water. No work was carried out until the early 1920s however, the branch opening on 20th July 1926. The most convenient way of travelling between Southampton and the Fawley district for most people is by using the Hythe ferry, so consequently passenger traffic along the branch was always negligible. The winter 1954/55 timetable, for example, advertised the grand total of two weekday trains to and from Southampton, with just one service on Sundays! These trains were timed to run for the benefit of workers travelling to Fawley. This meagre service was withdrawn from 14th February 1966, so the branch lasted for only 40 years as a passenger railway. The line is still very much in business however, carrying considerable oil traffic from Fawley. Here a pair of USA Class tank engines, Nos 30073 and 30064, take the Fawley branch at Totton with an enthusiasts' special train on 19th March 1966. *Neville Simms*

Viewed from the steps of Kimbridge Junction signal box, between Salisbury and Romsey, LSWR T9 4–4–0 No 30287 is seen passing the junction in July 1958 with a Salisbury to Portsmouth freight. The route on the right of the picture was the branch that ran up the River Test valley to Andover and was closed to passenger traffic on 7th September 1964. The line remained more or less intact for a number of years following closure and lifting was not completed until 1969. In 1948 Awbridge Sidings, near Kimbridge Junction, were used as a stabling point for locomotives awaiting scrapping at Eastleigh Works.
S.C Townroe/Colour-Rail

SALISBURY TO PORTSMOUTH

BR Standard Class 5MT No 73111 *King Uther* hauling the 10.25am Brighton to Plymouth train is seen near Bitterne on a snowy 28th December 1964. By this time Brighton shed had been closed and the steam motive power for this working was being supplied by the South Western Section. For a period, one of the SR's Co-Co electric locomotives was rostered to haul this train between Brighton and Chichester, so Plymouth-bound passengers would presumably have been hauled by three different types of traction – electric to Chichester, steam from there to Salisbury, and diesel onwards.
Mike Hudson

The crew of a motor boat in the foreground carry on with their tasks, apparently oblivious to the presence of a BR Standard Class 5MT and its train on the bridge. The unidentified Class 5MT was working a diverted Waterloo-bound express on 20th March 1966. This spot – the River Hamble bridge at Bursledon – was a popular photographic location which, owing to the regular movement of boats on the river, was almost guaranteed to produce a different picture on each visit. Unfortunately, the number of steam workings along the Fareham to Southampton route diminished when the local passenger trains were dieselised in 1957, and by the time of this picture very few regular steam workings remained. *Roy Hobbs*

Maunsell U Class 'Mogul' No 31793 is seen leaving Fareham with the 12.27pm Portsmouth & Southsea to Southampton Terminus train on 28th October 1962. Presumably steam traction was deputising for a non-available diesel unit. The train is correctly signalled for the Southampton direction. The other two signals on the gantry refer to the Eastleigh route for which there were two separate lines from Fareham, which merged about two miles or so beyond the town. The impressive semaphores were replaced by colour light signals, controlled by Eastleigh panel box, in June 1982. The train is leaving from the up main platform. In about 1970, however, the roadbridge at the eastern end of the station, a parapet of which is just discernible, was replaced by two separate spans to permit road widening and the opportunity was taken to ease the very tight curves at that end of the station. Henceforth, the up through trains used the outer face of the platform while the former up main line became an up bay, generally used by Eastleigh shuttle services.
Mike Hudson

This general view of Portsmouth & Southsea Station taken during September 1965 shows BR Standard Class 5MT No 73115 *King Pellinore* waiting to leave with an unidentified passenger train, possibly the Portsmouth portion of the Brighton to Plymouth through train. On the left another BR Standard engine can be seen at the head of a van train. The first station in the city, which opened on 14th June 1847, was on this site, but much to the frustration of Portsmouth's citizens it only offered services along the coast to Brighton, and not trains to London. In order to reach London they either had to go via Brighton or take the ferry to Gosport which connected with the LSWR's trains. Another twelve years elapsed before direct London to Portsmouth services were provided. Portsmouth & Southsea Station – known as Portsmouth Town from 1876 to 1921 – was rebuilt in 1866 with five terminal platforms and when the extension to Portsmouth Harbour was authorised an island platform was added at a higher level on the seaward side of the station. Surprisingly, the name Portsmouth Town is still used locally on street signs today, almost eighty years since it ceased to be used officially by the railway authorities! *Roy Hobbs*

This picture of Portsmouth Harbour Station's curving platforms shows BR Standard Class 4MT No 75074 awaiting departure with 11.26am inter-regional holiday train to the north on 1st July 1967, just over a week prior to the demise of SR steam. The first station on this spot – above the choppy waters of Portsmouth Harbour – was opened on 2nd October 1876 and proved a godsend to Victorian holiday-makers heading for the Isle of Wight, who no longer had to trudge through the town between their train and ferry journeys. The station originally had three platforms, and two more were added in 1903. By the 1930s the premises were in a dilapidated condition and underwent drastic reconstruction in 1936/37, when new facilities were provided, including a much enlarged roof area. Sadly, the new station lasted less than four years, being hit by German bombs in August 1940. Worse was to come, however – on the night of 10/11th January 1941 the Luftwaffe struck again, doing much further damage. After the end of hostilities the station was again rebuilt, and it reopened in June 1946. *Mike Hudson*

THE DIDCOT, NEWBURY & SOUTHAMPTON LINE

The Didcot, Newbury and Southampton Railway was an independently promoted line which was authorised in 1873 to construct a railway between Didcot and a junction with the LSWR near Micheldever. At that time, the LSWR was very unpopular in Southampton, and a deputation was sent to encourage the DNSR to seek an independent approach to the port and develop itself as a through route to the Midlands. In August 1882 the DNSR obtained additional powers for a direct route to Southampton with a terminus near the Royal Pier. Despite a chronic shortage of funds it eventually reached Winchester Cheesehill (later Chesil) station, opening on 4th May 1885. The DNSR was a small concern, however, and had to contend with the outright hostility of the mighty LSWR, which grudgingly allowed a connection between the DNSR and its main Southampton line to be installed at Shawford, this coming into use on 1st October 1891. Running powers were not granted, however, and at first engines were changed at Winchester. The DNSR traversed a sparsely populated area which offered little traffic potential, but even so between the wars there were, amazingly, through coaches to Glasgow, an experiment which did not last. During the Second World War the route was upgraded for military traffic between the Midlands and Southampton, and several new facilities and signal boxes were provided. Passenger traffic was withdrawn from 7th March 1960, but the line remained open for through freight traffic for some years afterwards, until that also ceased in August 1964. Here, BR Standard Class 4MT No 75005 is seen near Winchester Junction on 5th March 1960 hauling a Southampton to Didcot train formed of GWR rolling stock. *Trevor Owen*

This typical 1950s scene at Winchester Chesil Station shows GWR 2251 Class 0–6–0 No 3212 emerging from the tunnel at the north end of the station with a Southampton-bound train. Initially, as previously mentioned, the hostile LSWR insisted that engines must be changed at Winchester, but later, as traffic on the DNSR grew, through locomotive working was permitted from 1st October 1910 and GWR engines started to be seen in Southampton. Though worked by the GWR, the line remained independent until the grouping in 1923. After closure of the route, Chesil Station was used for a time on summer Saturdays to prevent Southampton to Winchester short workings from delaying main line traffic while reversing at Winchester City. *Colour-Rail*

A view of Whitchurch Town Station looking north towards Newbury, which was presumably taken shortly before closure, showing a fine display of neatly trimmed privet bushes, which the station staff no doubt tended during the long periods between trains. The initial plans of the DNSR Company envisaged a connection between its route and the LSWR Basingstoke to Salisbury line at Whitchurch. In the late 1870s, however, the DNSR was so short of funds that Parliamentary powers were sought to abandon the line south of Whitchurch, which could easily have become the line's southern terminus! *Gerald Daniels*

The DNSR remained open for freight traffic for some years following its closure to passengers and was undoubtedly a useful link between the West Midlands and Southampton. Perhaps the best known trains routed via the DNSR were the heavy oil workings between Fawley and Bromford Bridge, near Birmingham, but in late 1963 a decision was taken to reroute these trains via Basingstoke and Reading. The writing was clearly on the wall for the DNSR line, which was left with only a handful of trains in each direction on weekdays, despite being manned around the clock. The inevitable closure to all traffic came on 10th August 1964. The Railway Correspondence & Travel Society was obviously aware of the line's impending fate and arranged for its 'East Midlander No 7' Nottingham to Eastleigh rail tour to be routed via the DNSR. This train, which was formed of LMSR rolling stock, is seen near Burghclere on 9th May 1964, with Bulleid Pacific No 34038 *Lynton* in charge. *Roy Hobbs*

A charming view of the small country station at Burghclere on the last day of passenger services, showing GWR 4300 Class 2–6–0 No 6302 arriving with a Southampton Terminus to Didcot service. Note that the passenger train appears to be well patronised by enthusiasts enjoying a 'last day' trip over the line, but 'ordinary' passengers are conspicuous by their absence. The summer 1957 timetable reveals that only six weekday trains were advertised in each direction, most of which ran between Southampton and Newbury. Only one return train a day ran along the entire line, between Southampton and Didcot, a 56½-mile long journey which took just over 2½ hours. Almost needless to say, there was no service on Sundays. *Trevor Owen*

BR Standard Class 4MT 2–6–0 No 76062 approaches Burghclere at the head of a southbound freight train on 5th March 1960, just two days prior to the withdrawal of passenger traffic. *Trevor Owen*

THE MID HANTS LINE

A rare colour illustration of Itchen Abbas Station, on the now closed section of the Mid Hants Line west of Alresford. A local train, hauled by LSWR M7 Class 0–4–4T No 30125, is pulling away from the platform on the next stage of its journey towards Winchester. Prior to electrification of the line from Waterloo to Alton in July 1937, this route was served by some through trains from London to Eastleigh or Southampton. When the new electric services were introduced east of Alton, the Mid Hants found itself on the fringe of the electrified area and, much to the annoyance of local travellers, these through workings were replaced by a push-pull service operating between Alton and Eastleigh/Southampton. Virtually overnight the line's status had declined from a secondary through route to little more than a sleepy country branch line with a sparse service of purely local trains. One of the first M7 Class engines drafted to the new push-pull trains in 1937 was No 125 and, twenty years later as BR No 30125, this locomotive was still employed on these duties. Shortly after this shot was taken in 1957 the line was dieselised as part of the SR's Hampshire dieselisation scheme, and evocative scenes such as this became a thing of the past. *Neil Sprinks*

The Alresford signalman holds out the tablet to the driver of BR Class 5MT 4–6–0 No 73171, which was working the diverted 11.30am Waterloo to Weymouth train on 12th June 1966. At this time the Bournemouth line was frequently blocked for engineering works at weekends and the Mid Hants Line was often used as a diversionary route. Alresford Station is, of course, now the headquarters of the Mid Hants Railway, and as a result of their efforts this scene is very much the same today. The train has just emerged from a very deep chalk cutting, these being a feature of this line. *David Wigley*

Prior to the electrification of part of the Kent Coast routes in 1959 locomotives built by the SECR were generally confined to the South Eastern Section of the SR. The introduction of electric traction displaced a large number of steam locomotives however, many of which were either withdrawn or moved to other areas. An astonishing feature of the June 1959 reallocation list was the nominal *en masse* transfer to Nine Elms shed of no fewer than 106 engines displaced from the Kent Coast services! It was likely that many of these locomotives never reached Nine Elms and some were noted stored out of use at other sheds, probably never to work again. SECR L Class 4–4–0 No 31768 was one of the more fortunate locomotives which did work from Nine Elms on various mundane duties, although it is also likely to have spent long periods in store. On 18th September 1960 it was employed on part of an LCGB rail tour, which it worked between Ascot and Eastleigh via Alton. It is seen here passing Ropley, where the sight of an L Class locomotive was probably unprecedented. *Paul Leavens*

Trains travelling in an easterly direction on the Mid Hants
Line face a steep climb from Alresford to Medstead, with
gradients mostly at 1 in 80. The final 1¾-mile stretch from
beyond Ropley to a point just short of Medstead Station was
however, on an even steeper 1 in 60 gradient. Here, BR
Standard Class 4MT 2–6–4T No 80139 is seen piloting Bulleid
'Merchant Navy' Class Pacific No 35029 *Ellerman Lines* past
Ropley Station on 22nd May 1966. The train was the 9.54am
Weymouth to Waterloo express which was re-routed due to
track work between Winchester and Woking. Since this
photograph was taken this scene has changed out of all
recognition. Ropley is now the headquarters of the Mid Hants
Railway's locomotive department whose works now occupies
the former goods yard site in the foreground. *Roy Hobbs*

Trains travelling from Alton towards Winchester are faced with a formidable climb up the three miles long 1 in 60 gradient of Medstead Bank, which commences just over a mile from Alton Station. During the ascent trains rise 313 feet before reaching the summit of the line at Medstead, which is 652 feet above sea level and the highest station in southern England. Consequently the line was often referred to by enginemen as going 'Over the Alps'. To say the least, it was a testing route and not one for faint-hearted enginemen or 'clapped out' locomotives! Naturally, it was a popular route for rail tours and in this view, taken on 9th January 1966, gleaming Maunsell S15 Class No 30837 creates a stirring image as it does battle with the 1 in 60 incline of Medstead Bank. This tour, advertised as the last working of an S15 Class engine, was actually a relief to the main tour which took place, in extremely snowy conditions, a week later. Two Urie-designed representatives of this class are currently preserved on the Mid Hants Railway, so it is still possible to travel behind engines of this class along this stretch of line! *Neville Simms*

For many years Dugald Drummond's 700 Class 0–6–0s, introduced in 1897, could be seen on Mid Hants Line freight workings and in this classic picture No 30350 is depicted entering Medstead & Four Marks with an Alton bound train in 1957. In about 1953 these engines were reportedly displaced from these duties by Q Class locomotives, but in 1956 Alton's turntable had to be taken out of use and a rearrangement of the engine diagrams was necessary, which resulted in the welcome reappearance of the 700s, or 'Black Motors' as they were universally called by footplatemen. Today, Medstead is a beautifully maintained intermediate station on the Mid Hants Railway, and is probably busier than at any time in its career. *Neil Sprinks*

The 9.33am Waterloo to Bournemouth train, diverted due to engineering operations on the main line, slows to a halt in Alton Station on 18th September 1966. Motive power is provided by a decidedly dirty Bulleid Light Pacific No 34023 *Blackmore Vale*, which was later preserved and can be seen today on the Bluebell Railway in Sussex. It is recorded that No 34023's crew obtained the services of an assisting engine for the steep climb of Medstead Bank. Regrettably, from the steam enthusiasts' point of view, the pilot was BRCW Type 3 (later Class 33) diesel electric No D6577, and this continued as far as Winchester. The first railway to reach Alton was a branch from Guildford which opened in July 1852, the direct route from London via Pirbright not being opened until 1870. The line westwards to Winchester was proposed by the Alton, Alresford and Winchester Railway Company in 1860 and an Act of Parliament sanctioning the route was passed in June 1861. The line eventually opened on 2nd October 1865, by which time the original company had changed its name to the Mid Hants Railway Company (MHR). Initially the LSWR was hostile to the MHR, but relations gradually improved and in 1880 the LSWR was granted an option to purchase the line. Four years later, on 30th June 1884, the LSWR acquired the whole of the MHR's assets. *David Wigley*

THE GOSPORT BRANCH

On a sunny 20th February 1966 a rail tour passes the former Fort Brockhurst Station, heading towards Fareham with Maunsell N Class 'Mogul' No 31411 in charge. By this time the N Class had been reduced to a handful of examples, which were consequently in great demand for specials. It was still possible to travel behind a Maunsell 'Mogul' in regular service on the 7.30am Woking to Basingstoke passenger train, which was diagrammed to be worked by an N Class locomotive from Guildford shed. No 31411 was withdrawn in April 1966 after over 32 years' service. Amazingly, in November 1952, Fort Brockhurst Station had a Royal visitor when it was used by HM the Queen (then Princess Elizabeth) when she was *en route* to the Royal Naval Air Station at Lee-on-Solent.
J. Spencer Gilks

The LSWR obtained the Royal Assent for a line from Eastleigh to Fareham, with branches to Gosport and Portsmouth, in June 1839. The line was intended to provide the citizens of those places with rail access to London. Portsmouth Corporation favoured a direct line from Portsmouth to the Capital however, but was placated when it emerged that construction of the Gosport branch would not jeopardise the building of a direct line. Despite also being opposed by the Admiralty, work on the Gosport line went ahead and it was opened on 29th November 1841. No building work was undertaken on the Portsmouth line at this time, but the LSWR and LBSCR later agreed to have a joint line into Portsmouth and this opened in October 1848. The opening of this route meant an immediate reduction in status for the Gosport branch. After the Second World War passenger traffic dwindled to such an extent that closure occurred in 1953, though the line remained open for goods traffic. Towards the end of SR steam the Gosport branch was regularly visited by enthusiasts' specials, and these appear to have been the only trains on the branch that were photographed in colour. Here, Q1 Class 0-6-0 No 33006, hauling a Locomotive Club of Great Britain rail tour on 19th March 1966, is depicted near Rowner heading towards Fareham after visiting Gosport. *Neville Simms*

Photographed on 20th February 1966, N Class No 31411 is seen awaiting departure from Gosport with the Southern Counties Touring Society special train which is also seen in the picture on the opposite page. The roof of the former Gosport Station – which is a magnificent building of considerable architectural interest – can be glimpsed in the background. *Paul Leavens*

There were various early plans to give Windsor, Ascot and Aldershot a direct route to the South Coast and most schemes involved a route from either the Farnham or Alton areas to Fareham via West Meon. Eventually, on 3rd June 1897, the LSWR obtained an Act of Parliament for the 'Meon Valley Railway' which would connect Alton and Fareham, and provide a through route from Waterloo to Gosport and Stokes Bay, from where a ferry service operated to the Isle of Wight. In addition, it also offered an alternative line from London to Portsmouth. The promoters optimistically envisaged that the route would develop into a busy main line and with this in mind a double track formation was constructed, but only one track was laid. Long platforms were also built at all stations. The Meon Valley Line opened on 1st June 1903, but it soon became clear that the line, which served a thinly populated area of scattered rural communities, was never going to achieve the main line status originally anticipated. The route closed to passengers in February 1955, so it is fortunate that a few colour pictures were taken. In this shot T9 Class No 30732 is seen shunting at Droxford in early 1955. *S.C. Townroe/Colour-Rail*

THE MEON VALLEY LINE

The last scheduled passenger trains ran on the Meon Valley Line on Saturday 5th February 1955, but on the following day a rail tour organised by the Railway Correspondence & Travel Society travelled over the route. The special halted at West Meon to enable photographs to be taken, but unfortunately the train stopped with the locomotives positioned in a deep cutting – not the most suitable arrangement for the photographers! Here, dozens of enthusiasts are seen risking life and limb as they scramble for a suitable position on the side of the cutting. Motive power was provided by a pair of T9 Class 4–4–0s, Nos 30301 and 30732. *Trevor Owen*

THE BISHOPS WALTHAM BRANCH

The 3½-mile long branch from Botley, on the Fareham to Eastleigh line, to Bishops Waltham was opened by the Bishops Waltham Railway Company on 1st June 1863, but the line was soon absorbed by the LSWR. There was an intermediate station, Durley Halt, which was opened from 23rd December 1909. The initial timetable advertised six weekday and three Sunday trains, but in 1869 the service was reduced to four trains on weekdays only. An improvement was made in 1889 when the number of trains was increased to seven, and a further enhancement occurred in 1907 when railmotors, which lasted about ten years, were introduced, and these provided twelve weekday trains. Sunday services were reintroduced from this time with six or seven trips being provided until 1918. Economies were made in that year, the Sunday timetable being reduced to four trains and these were withdrawn permanently in 1931. The weekday service had been trimmed to nine trains by 1925 and was further cut back, to only six workings, in the final years. The line was vulnerable to road competition and passenger services were withdrawn from 2nd January 1933. Bishops Waltham boasted an engine shed, which was demolished in 1931, and also a signal box which was closed in December 1935, with all points and signals being worked by hand from that time. Perhaps the most interesting facet of the branch was the short industrial line at Bishops Waltham which served a brick and tile works, until about 1946. There was also a siding serving a brewery. Freight trains continued to run to Bishops Waltham until 30th April 1962 and during the line's declining years a number of rail tours visited the route. The distinctive Bishops Waltham Station building is portrayed in this shot, which was taken on 16th September 1959. *Alan Jarvis*

Most of the Portsmouth to Brighton West Coast Line (not to be confused with the better known London to Glasgow route of the same name!) is located in Sussex, and therefore geographically outside the scope of this album. In addition, it could be said with considerable justification that the West Coast Line loses its identity when the Portsmouth Direct Line is joined, just outside Havant Station. In this shot Bulleid Pacific No 34101 *Hartland*, hauling a Brighton to Bournemouth West train, is seen passing over the junction with the latter route on a sunny 4th November 1962. No 34101, which was shedded at Brighton at that time, is in magnificent, highly polished condition, for which Brighton shed was justly famed. *Mike Hudson*

THE WEST COAST LINE

The sight of two LBSCR A1X Class 0–6–0Ts, universally known as 'Terriers', double-heading an empty stock train from Fratton to Havant prior to spending a day working the Hayling Island branch, must have been repeated many times over the years. This picture, however, was taken on 3rd November 1963, the last day of services along the branch, so this was the very last time such a scene could be witnessed. Here Nos 32670 and 32636 are illustrated approaching Bedhampton Halt with the empty stock of the Havant to Hayling Island section of the Locomotive Club of Great Britain's 'Hayling Farewell' rail tour on that date. By the time of this photograph the combined ages of these sprightly veterans was a mere 182 years and, almost needless to say, both were purchased for preservation after withdrawal by BR. The coach formed immediately behind the engines appears to be No S1000S, an experimental non-corridor vehicle made of glass-fibre, which was often, though mistakenly, referred to as the 'plastic' coach. *Roy Hobbs*

THE HAYLING ISLAND BRANCH

The 4½-mile long, single-track Hayling Railway was opened throughout from Havant to South Hayling (renamed Hayling Island in 1892) on 16th July 1867, a short section to Langston having opened for goods traffic a few years earlier. The Company had obtained an Act of Parliament in July 1860, but there was a long delay in opening the branch. This is explained by the fact that it originally chose to route the line down the western shore of the island, on a separate embankment which involved reclaiming part of Langston Harbour mudflats. Those who proposed this rather strange and unwise course had not bargained for the erosion caused by the tide in Langston Harbour, which removed embankment spoil almost as fast as the contractor could deposit it! This serious miscalculation brought the Hayling company to the verge of collapse, but in 1866 a new chairman was appointed who revived interest in the project and, most importantly, altered the course of the line on to a more practical site. The line was leased to the LBSCR in 1871, the Hayling company remaining nominally independent. It will be best remembered for the LBSCR 'Terrier' 0–6–0Ts, which were the only engines permitted to work the branch owing to a severe weight restriction on Langston bridge. The line conveyed huge numbers of holiday-makers during the summer period, with a very intensive service being timetabled, especially at weekends. Here, 'Terrier' No 32646 is depicted entering Langston Halt on 16th September 1959 with a train bound for Hayling Island. The small station here, which was located where the line crossed the main road to the island, was originally named 'Langstone' but the LBSCR changed it to Langston in 1873. *Alan Jarvis*

A down train, headed by 'Terrier' No 32650, rumbles across Langston Bridge at high tide on 15th August 1963. The short two-coach train is made up of a BR Standard non-corridor coach, formed immediately behind the engine, plus a Maunsell brake vehicle on the rear. No 32650 probably has one of the most colourful histories of any locomotive featured in this book. It was built as LBSCR No 50 *Whitechapel* in December 1876, but it appeared destined to have only a brief working life when, in 1905, it was included in the LBSCR's withdrawal programme. At about that time, however, the 'Brighton' company decided to introduce motor-trains and No 50 was fortunate enough to be selected for use on these new services. At the Grouping in 1923 No B650 (as No 50 had become) was based at Fratton shed. The next major landmark in the engine's career occurred in 1930 when No B650 was sent to the Isle of Wight as No W9 *Fishbourne*. The heyday of the 'Terriers' on the island came to an end in 1936 when Class 02s took over most of their remaining turns, and W9 returned to the mainland. It was overhauled at Eastleigh Works, repainted in lined green, renumbered 515S in the departmental list and despatched to Lancing Works, where it joined its sister No 680S on pilot duty. It remained at Lancing until November 1953 when it was released from its chores there and returned to normal running stock as No 32650. It then spent much of its remaining ten years of life on BR working the Hayling Island branch and, in March 1963, was the final 'Terrier' to be granted a general overhaul. Following withdrawal in November 1963, No 32650 was purchased by the London Borough of Sutton and earmarked for display at their new civic centre. The 'Terrier' was moved to the Kent & East Sussex Railway for 'temporary' storage in 1964, prior to the intended transfer to Sutton. This has never taken place, however, and this remarkable little engine, which was slated for withdrawal as long ago as 1905, is still resident on the K&ESR at the time of writing. *R.C. Riley*

Hayling Island Station is the setting for this early 1960s picture of LBSCR 'Terrier' 0–6–0T No 32646 and its short train, which is formed of a Maunsell brake vehicle plus a BR Standard compartment carriage. The engine is presumably about to run around its train before returning to Havant. The station building at Hayling Island was noteworthy for its half-timbered construction, some distinctive herringbone pattern brickwork and red tiled roof. The platform was constructed entirely of brick. There had even been a small engine shed, but this was closed in 1894 and subsequently demolished. A small coal stage, built of sleepers, was located adjacent to the run around loop, but there were no watering facilities. The small goods yard at Hayling Island boasted a red brick goods shed and office built in the early 1900s as the result of an upsurge in traffic. There was also a small loading dock. Freight facilities were officially available until the line's demise, but were latterly very little used. *Gerald Daniels*

The last day of services on the Hayling Island branch will always be remembered for this absolutely stunning sunset. Need any more be said? *Gerald Daniels*

THE PORTSMOUTH DIRECT LINE

The earliest railway in the Portsmouth area opened in 1841 but that, as mentioned elsewhere in this album, only served Gosport. The citizens of Portsmouth – which had a population of 54,000 at that time – were obliged to cross the harbour on a ferry in order to board a train which offered a connection to London. Two schemes were proposed in 1844 which would have given Portsmouth a direct link to the Capital, but neither obtained Parliamentary approval. The Guildford to Godalming section of the proposed Guildford, Chichester & Portsmouth Railway was, however, sanctioned in 1846. At the same time Parliament also approved the Direct London & Portsmouth Company's plans, but these later foundered due to lack of finance. This situation provided the incentive for a 'contractor's group' to construct a link from Godalming to Havant, the former town then being the terminus of a branch from Guildford. This new line would provide the direct, faster route to London that the people of Portsmouth had long desired. Led by the celebrated railway contractor Thomas Brassey, the Portsmouth Railway Company obtained Parliamentary approval for their scheme on 8th July 1853. The line, which was cheaply built with many tight curves and heavy gradients, opened in 1859. Fearful that their competitors might try to encroach on their territory, the LSWR decided to lease the line, which was initially only a single track, and doubling was completed in 1878. After electrification in July 1937, the Portsmouth Direct Line was hardly a paradise for steam enthusiasts, but the occasional diversion of Waterloo to Bournemouth/ Weymouth services did sometimes provide worthwhile opportunities for steam photographers. Here, Bulleid Light Pacific No 34031 *Torrington* is pictured leaving Havant in charge of the 9.25am Bournemouth West to Waterloo train on 28th October 1962. No 34031 was a relatively early casualty, being withdrawn in February 1965. *Mike Hudson*

In this portrait of the eastern end of Havant Station taken on 4th November 1962, unrebuilt Bulleid Pacific No 34006 *Bude* is seen getting into its stride with the diverted 9.25am Bournemouth West to Waterloo train, the same working as that in the previous shot. This spot was the scene of an acrimonious dispute between the LSWR and LBSCR which occurred in 1858 shortly before the Portsmouth Direct route was opened. The company which built the line had been granted running powers by Parliament over the Havant to Portsmouth stretch, but when the LSWR leased the line, and took over the running powers, the rival LBSCR referred the matter to arbitration. The LSWR chose to take matters into its own hands however, and advised the LBSCR that it would send a freight train down the Portsmouth Direct Line on 28th December 1858, and intended to operate regular services thereafter. The LBSCR retaliated by chaining a locomotive to the track, apparently causing the LSWR's train to enter Havant on the wrong line. A considerable altercation ensued, which is sometimes dubbed the 'Battle of Havant'. Later the LSWR obtained an injunction restraining the 'Brighton' company and through running from London commenced on 24th January 1859. *Mike Hudson*

The Portsmouth Direct Line is, as previously stated, extremely steeply graded, with some sections inclined at 1 in 80. Here BR Standard Class 5MT No 73114 *Etarre*, heading a diverted London-bound express, raises the echoes as it attacks the long climb from Havant to Buriton Tunnel. After Buriton there is a downhill run to Petersfield, but shortly afterwards the eleven-mile long ascent to Haslemere begins, much of it being at 1 in 100 or steeper, so there would have been little respite for the fireman. This view was photographed north of Rowlands Castle on 20th March 1966. *Trevor Owen*

A London-bound express, in charge of Bulleid Light Pacific No 34024 *Tamar Valley*, drifts down from Buriton Tunnel towards Petersfield on 20th March 1966. Note the short wooden platform which was presumably built for the convenience of BR staff working on the line, or in the tunnel. No 34024's chief claim to fame was probably its appearance on the down 'Bournemouth Belle' on 5th July 1967, a few days before the sad demise of SR steam. It was the last recorded appearance of steam traction on the down working of the 'Belle'. *Trevor Owen*

THE LONGMOOR MILITARY RAILWAY

The Longmoor Military Railway was operated as a training school for the railway troops of the Royal Engineers and was one of the largest independent railway systems in the country. The section between Longmoor and Bordon was built between 1905 and 1909 and was originally known as the Woolmer Instructional Military Railway. In 1933 an extension to Liss, on the Waterloo to Portsmouth route, was opened and the name of the establishment was altered to the Longmoor Military Railway. There was a substantial layout at Longmoor and this picture, taken when a rail tour visited the line in April 1966, provides a panoramic view of some of the line's equipment and facilities. The line to Liss crossed the main line and locomotive shed approach tracks on a bridge which is visible on the extreme right. The large building in the centre of the shot is the diesel locomotive repair depot, above which the roof of the signal school is visible. The 'main line' track bears right between the carriage shed and the signal school. On the extreme left the steam locomotive shed can just be discerned. The engine in the foreground is No 600 *Gordon*, which was the flagship of the Longmoor fleet at that time.
R.C. Riley

Two 'Austerity' 0–6–0 saddle tank locomotives pose for the photographer at Longmoor on 30th April 1966. They are Longmoor Military Railway Nos 195 and 196 which were both built by Hunslet of Leeds in 1953 (Works Nos 3795/6). A total of 377 locomotives of this type were constructed for the Ministry of Supply between 1942 and 1946. After the end of the Second World War further engines were built, including the examples seen here. These locomotives may not have been particularly attractive, but what they may have lacked in appearance was compensated for by their good steaming characteristics, abundant power and ability to negotiate sharp curves. They were used at industrial sites virtually all over Great Britain and became the National Coal Board's staple motive power for shunting at collieries. Today they are still a very common sight throughout the country at various preservation centres. *R.C. Riley*

No 30064 was one of a number of USA Class 0–6–0Ts which remained in service when SR steam traction came to an end in July 1967 and was subsequently purchased privately for preservation. It was initially based on a section of the former Meon Valley Line at Droxford and later on the Longmoor Military Railway at Liss on which enthusiasts hoped to establish a preserved railway. The scheme failed due to opposition from local residents and the stock was dispersed, the bulk of the items moving to the Bluebell Railway in Sussex. One of the last events at Liss before the site was cleared of preserved stock was the filming of 'Young Winston', in which No 30064 featured disguised as a South African Railway's locomotive. It may seem rather strange that an engine built in America, and modified for use in Great Britain, should be used in this role, but that is what happened! The engine was fitted with a cow catcher and its sidetanks adorned with appropriate initials. The USA tank engine is seen at Liss during filming operations on 14th October 1971 with part of the suitably modified Liss LMR station building just visible on the left of the picture. *David Wigley*

THE BORDON BRANCH

Left The 4½-mile long Bordon branch, which ran from Bentley on the Aldershot to Alton line, to the village of Bordon, was built primarily to connect Woolmer Forest army camp with the National railway network. It therefore differs from other branch lines included in this book because heavy military traffic was its principal source of income, and not local civilian passenger business. In order to cater for the military, Bordon Station was built with four platforms, each capable of accommodating a ten coach train. The branch was constructed under a Light Railway Order which allowed ungated level crossings – the order being obtained in October 1902. Work started in mid-1904 and construction proceeded with commendable speed, the line opening on 11th December 1905. In this picture LSWR M7 0–4–4T No 30110, with a wisp of steam escaping from its safety valves, propels a two-coach push-pull train towards Bentley on 15th September 1957, the penultimate day of public passenger services along the branch. Following withdrawal of the public passenger trains the Bordon branch remained in use for army freight traffic for some years afterwards, but this dwindled away and the line eventually closed completely on 4th April 1966. At least that was the official closure date, but the last train, a Railway Correspondence & Travel Society rail tour hauled by WD 2–10–0 No 600 *Gordon*, ran some weeks later, on 30th April 1966. *Trevor Owen*

Above A Bordon to Bentley train, or 'Bordon Flyer' as the train was known locally, leaves Kingsley Halt on 22nd July 1956. LSWR 0–4–4T No 30027 is propelling at the rear. The halt opened in 1906, some months after the line, and the LSWR – anticipating residential development in the immediate area – purchased sufficient land to enable a proper station and goods yard to be built. Unfortunately, this did not materialise and Kingsley Halt retained its extremely basic 'facilities', which merely consisted of a simple wooden platform equipped with a noticeboard, station nameboard, an electric lamp and a seat! No covered accommodation was provided for the tiny number of passengers who used the halt. *Trevor Owen*

THE READING TO REDHILL LINE

Maunsell N Class 'Mogul' No 31872 hauls a local working along the Reading to Redhill line near Farnborough on 6th September 1962. The train comprised a set of four carriages which, like the engine pulling them, are also of Maunsell design. The bridge in the background carries the Waterloo to Bournemouth main line over the SECR route. The enginemen were distracted by the 'Red Arrows' apparently rehearsing for the Farnborough Air Show. *Derek Penney*

Maunsell U Class 'Mogul' No 31799 rolls into Farnborough North Station with an unidentified Reading to Guildford working on 9th September 1964. This station lies very close to the Blackwater river which forms the boundary between Hampshire and Surrey, so this shot only just qualifies for inclusion in this album. Between Farnborough North and North Camp, the next station along the line towards Guildford, the river meanders underneath the line, so the latter station is outside the scope of the book, but only by a few yards. *Alan Jarvis*

No 31799 pulls away from Farnborough North Station with the train seen in the previous picture. This locomotive was originally built by Armstrong Whitworth as K Class 2–6–4T No A799 *River Test* in 1925. This class was involved in a series of derailments shortly after its introduction, including the Sevenoaks accident, which occurred on 24th August 1927, involving considerable loss of life. It was therefore decided to rebuild the entire class as 2–6–0 tender engines, No A799 being converted at Ashford Works in July 1928. The U Class remained in active use until 1966. *Alan Jarvis*